AT HOME WITH
Roses

Text by
JEANINE LARMOTH

HEARST BOOKS · NEW YORK

LIBRARY OF CONGRESS CATALOGING-IN-PUBLICATION DATA
Larmoth, Jeanine.
Victoria, at home with roses / text by Jeanine Larmoth. — 1st ed.
p. cm.
ISBN 0-688-14474-8
1. Roses in art. 2. Decoration and ornament—Plant forms.
3. Interior decoration. I. Victoria (New York, N.Y.) II. Title
NK2115.5.P49L37 1997   96-54305
747'. 9—DC21   CIP

PRINTED IN SINGAPORE

First Edition

1 2 3 4 5 6 7 8 9 10

FOR VICTORIA—

Nancy Lindemeyer Editor-in-Chief

Susan Maher Art Director

John Mack Carter President, Hearst Magazine Enterprises

EDITED BY Laurie Orseck   DESIGNED BY Susi Oberhelman

PRODUCED BY SMALLWOOD & STEWART, INC., NEW YORK CITY

C O

N T E N T S

FOREWORD

In this book we are promising you a rose garden of ideas you will never forget. Whether you decide to decorate a whole room with rose-covered wall coverings or simply pick a tea-stained fabric with the look of old English garden roses for a bedroom chair, you'll find, as I have, how you never tire of such friendly decorating.

Roses bloom on these pages in so many ways, from freshly cut bouquets to projects you can do yourself to bring the joy and exuberance of roses to your everyday life. And naturally there are rose gardens, too, to inspire your own plantings.

When I was a youngster, roses climbed all over the fence around our house and over the arbor to the garden gate. I know it sounds picturesque ~ and it was. They were just "garden-variety" roses, but I loved them. I also remember the room at the tip-top of my grandmother's house all decorated in roses. In one of my first homes, I filled the walls in a gabled room with old rose prints, very reasonable to collect, to give me the spirit of that inviting room. Guests always enjoyed staying in my "rose garden."

We hope with this book that you will find yourself completely at home with roses, and that your imagination will flower as you turn the pages. Entering our rose garden will be just like sitting on the porch on a summer evening with the scent of old-fashioned roses all about you, and you'll be creating new memories for your family and friends. A rose, I think, is not just a rose, it is a treasure.

NANCY LINDEMEYER
Editor-in-Chief
Victoria *Magazine*

INTRODUCTION

For the rose lover, there can never be enough roses. There can never be hours enough to breathe in their fragrance, enough tables to put them on, chairs and sofas to pile with rose-embroidered pillows, bowls to heap with their scented petals. There are not walls enough to paper with their patterns, not rooms enough to tint from a rose-colored palette. There are not enough beds in the garden to plant with roses or arbors to entwine. The rose both satisfies a need and creates a hunger for more.

Of all the myths throughout history that attempt to explain the flower's hold on us, none are lovelier than these: that the rose was born from the smile of the mischievous Cupid; that the rose fell from Aurora's dawn-streaked hair as she combed it; that roses burst from the foam that covered Venus when she was born from the sea. Since those legendary days, the rose has never ceased to inspire ~ in verse, art, architecture, music, dance, flights of fancy. It is a cherished symbol, the perfect tribute.

A rose is a floral world in itself. It is nourishment for the senses. To the eye, the rose offers radiance of hue and subtlety of form, carrying with it a sense of comfort and security. Its scent, warm and delicate as the notes of the flute, is a silken ribbon that seems to draw the house together into a single, serene space.

The rose also best responds to every emotion, every occasion. It becomes a poem for the lover, eloquence for the shy, a precious gift for everyone. For the gardener, the attentions the rose requires ~ the faithful watering, the snipping of spent blossoms as the light fades ~ provide her with longed-for moments of balance.

For these reasons, we seek places and times to increase the number of roses in our lives. This we accomplish not only by planting more shrubs or filling more vases, but by finding ever new ways of exploring the rose as motif. And in so doing, we bring to our homes a measure of the boundless grace that is the rose.

Rose Pot-pourri

To a basin of dried scented roses

add a handful of dried

knotted Marjoram, lemon thyme,

Rosemary, Lavender

flowers all well dried, the rind

of one lemon and one

orange dried to powder, six dried

bay leaves, half an ounce

of bruised cloves, a teaspoon

of Allspice. Mix well

together and stir occasionally.

dated 1895

THE DECOR

ROSES ARE, OR OUGHT TO BE, part of every day of a rose lover's life. They embellish each moment; they bring the sense of occasion to what might otherwise seem ordinary days. A cluster of roses on the tea table, pots of miniature roses in a sunny kitchen window ~ these are touches that transform the taken-for-granted into the special. The serenity the rose promises, through its shape, its fragrance, the coolness of its blossoms, is the atmosphere many of us would like to prevail in our homes and in our private time. Even at its most generous and seemingly abandoned ~ petals loose and abundant ~ the rose honors the intimate and personal, the hours spent apart from the world, when only the tick of the clock sounds in the room.

Because of this sense of privacy, the bedroom is perhaps the most desirable room to turn into a rose chamber. When

ATIVE ROSE

we waken beneath a flower-strewn canopy, on patterned or embroidered sheets, on pillowcases appliquéd with tiny, silken rosebuds, it is as if we have slept in the heart of the rose. The day's first light may be imprinted with the flower's emblem on draperies or lace curtains. A chaise longue upholstered in flowered linen or cotton, draped with a rosy-hued throw, becomes an invitation to reverie in the afternoon. Dried rosebuds ringed round a lamp's shade make the light seem softer; framing a beloved photograph on the bedside table, they make it dearer still. A scented candle gives the fragrance of roses to the evening; rose-colored lights cast a glow over every corner of the room.

Bedroom walls easily become giant canvases dedicated to the rose. They may be painted with flamboyant, larger-than-life roses or papered in a dainty overall pattern, the border festooned with roses, as a Victorian or Edwardian bedroom would have

been. The walls might also be painted one of the hundred dream-provoking tones that match a rose catalogue's poetic descriptions: the color of cream, peach, and apricot; coral, mauve, pale pink, dusky rose; touches of lavender, violet.

The ceiling and walls of a hallway can become a country path, painted with trompe l'oeil treillage and exuberant blossoms that seem about to shower those who pass with a deluge of petals. Even in a tailored room, where rose colors could be excessive, monochromatic patterns or white floral shapes embossed on the wallpaper or embroidered on the upholstery will make the rose's presence felt. Artists' prints, suspended from rose velvet ribbons, bring the flower before us. The prints might be of Redouté's classic rose portraits; they could be a collection of watercolors or antique prints that recall pleasant hours spent browsing in antique shops or book stalls.

A beloved family photograph poised beside the bed, for a last look at night and a first look in the morning, becomes more precious still when set off by a bouquet of tumbling roses and a single triumphant bloom in an antique cup.

The bathroom, too, can become a garden of colors and fragrances. Towels might harbor a bouquet of rose tints, patterns, or borders; hand towels might become an excuse to display fragile confections of linen embroidered with tiny buds. The linen cupboard is a natural haven for sachets stowed between sheets and towels. The cotton shower curtain might be appliquéd with flowers cut from a scrap of printed fabric.

Everything should conspire to scent the air with roses as well. Soap tablets in tea rose, moss rose, or bois de rose add their floral notes. An open shelf or a small antique table can hold a basket or bowl of potpourri. A bathroom shelf or two might be arrayed with rosy delights for the bath and after: rose water to soften and sooth the skin, rose bath salts to soften the water, English creams and lotions that make you feel beautiful simply smoothing them on. Rose

The same crowded sense to be found in a garden fills a room where roses invade every corner. Here, the Limoges demitasse, cotton tapestry covering the chair, Victorian petit point rug, bouquet of fresh-cut flowers from the garden, even a screen handpainted with giant roses transform a sitting room into a rosy alcove.

fragrances can stand ready to be daubed on on summer mornings or when dressing to meet a friend for tea. In the middle of winter, rose-laden perfumes bring back the radiant light of summer.

To turn a nursery or a bedroom for a little girl into a fairyland of roses, the walls could be painted a barely discernible blush of pink or stenciled with garlands. A quilt in one of the patterns that kept our ancestors busy at their quilting bees ~ World's Rose, Cherokee Rose, or Rosebud ~ might dress the bed. An artist's palette, garden flowers, or a florist's display can inspire colors to be brushed on walls and furniture. A splash of roses might, for pure delight, be set to dancing on the ceiling.

A tier of dried pink roses encircles taller red ones in a low glass bowl swagged with ormolu. The rose motif is echoed in the delicacy of the rose-painted cabinet and the painting on the wall. Overleaf: A classic antique French screen covered with handfuls of roses gets subtle but flowery reinforcement from an appliquéd pillow and embroidered throw.

The rose as theme draws everything in a house into harmony, not only visually but spiritually. Opening the door to a house where roses reign is like opening the door on a dream. ❧

Rose-patterned wallpaper

warms and enriches

even the darkest corner, opposite.

To keep a tiny room

private but still inviting, a soft,

rose-printed drape

takes the place of a door, left.

Windows seem to promise garden views with carved-rose tiebacks,

above left, or tea-dyed Chinese paper ones fluttering on a

braided cord, above right. If the drapery is sheer, so much the better:

A rose-printed curtain, opposite, blurry as a watercolor,

softly diffuses the light; fresh roses, their petals swirling in four parts

as old roses often do, carry on the curtain's pink tones.

Nothing makes a room
"hum with home," as Harriet Beecher
Stowe might have said,
more than mounds of rose-patterned
cushions. Blossoms nod on
old cushions, opposite, and on a sofa
covered with palest flowers
that seem to have faded with time.
Less expected are rounded
petit-point roses on sharp-angled
plaid, above left, in the manner
of nineteenth-century Berlin woolwork,
and a boldly modern rose
needlepoint, below left. Overleaf:
Summer lingers forever in a pale pink
room dressed with a rattan
settee and softened with cushions
of floral cretonne.

In swags or garlands, nosegays or simple sprays, roses woven

on carpets and rugs give us the sense of treading

lightly in a field of flowers. Whether the rug is a Savonnerie

or Aubusson from France, an antique Chinese, above,

or contemporary needlepoint, opposite, the interpretation of the roses

themselves will help make a room elegant or homey.

A wardrobe filled with
treasure too beautiful to conceal,
opposite, at home in either
bath or bedroom, may hold perfumed
soaps as well as every type
of rose-sprigged bedding: pillow
shams, sheets, duvets.
Sweet dreams come easily to those
who sleep on rose-covered
pillows, above and below left,
particularly those with rose sachets
tucked beneath them.

A dainty table painted with roses, opposite, becomes

a unique little dressing vanity. The bold rug, fairly blooming

with flowers, completes this charming vignette.

In an all-white bathroom, above, rose-bordered towels

provide just the right dash of color.

ENGLISH COTTAGE STYLE

The garden of an English cottage might be called the cradle of the rose. It is there that the flower is most tenderly nurtured, most truly at home. Roses are grown elsewhere, roses are loved elsewhere, and most of the great roses originated in other parts of the world, but it is the Englishman's passion for gardening and for the rose that have made the cottage garden the ideal. In it, for want of space, rose bushes are overplanted, happily crammed together, and allowed to encroach on tousled flower beds. This very lack of space and the untidy profusion of the planting that brought the rose to its finest flowering is what writer Vita Sackville-West

called "probably the prettiest form of gardening ever achieved in [England]."

In the cottage garden, pressed to find room, the rose clambered over weathered garden walls; it shielded, in tangled hedges, the cabbages, leeks, and runner beans, the currants and gooseberries of the kitchen garden. Scented roses were also encouraged to climb up the cottage walls so that an open window, a door left ajar, meant an intoxicating breath of perfume.

The same wash of scent and beauty, the same freedom from constraint, the same careless proliferation that rules the garden turned the interior of the cottage into a garden as well. A lavish bunch of disheveled roses might be thrust in an old coffeepot, combined with a branch of raspberries in a Mason jar, pressed into the same anything-that-comes-to-hand one might reach for in a rented summer cottage by the sea.

Roses not only overflowed the cottage, they contributed its dominant decorating motif. Like the flowers in the garden, they crowded every inch of space. No corner

Daybeds and sofas become fields of dreams, bathed in light and roses, this page and overleaf. Heapings of pillows transform them into cosy rooms, where little guests may pile up for a reading of "Wind in the Willows." By the magical addition of a lacy cloth and rose-ringed china on the table beside it, the daybed may also serve as a very private place for tea for one.

Breakfast in bed, English-cottage-style, includes a stack of rose-strewn chintz pillows borrowed from the sitting room; a tea cozy, its pattern borrowed from old tapestry, and a tussie-mussie freshly fetched from the garden. The walls, of course, are papered with roses.

could fail to be improved by the rose, no object was too small to bear its image. Roses bloomed on everything from the tiniest thimble in the sewing basket to the tapestry and needlepoint cushions on the sofa. Blowsy blossoms nodded on every chair, in paintings on the walls, on scrap screens, on teapots and quilted cosies. Plates looped with painted roses lined the open shelves of the Welsh dresser. The flower garlanded pitchers and basins ready for the morning toilette; ribboned the bedroom wallpaper, covered hatboxes with patterned paper or fabric, the hats themselves balancing rings of roses or a single wanton bloom.

Roses added an extra sense of comfort to chintz-covered easy chairs; skirted dressing tables and bedspreads; shut out winter darkness on heavy draperies. Scatter rugs and carpets were wreathed with flowers. Near the sofa, rose catalogues and books lay on small tables with rose inlays in the wood. The covers of old photograph albums bore embossed roses. Other precious albums

held old family postcards embellished with roses, sweet sayings, and dear signatures. The cheering light glowed through a lampshade covered in a decoupage of roses.

From this decorative bouquet comes the vision of the rose-covered cottage. So often has it been drawn in literature and art that it has become synonymous with an earthly paradise, a universal dream desired by all, improbable yet always yearned for. Inside thick whitewashed walls, a fire crackles in the fireplace; a dog, his head between his paws, drowses on the hearth; and roses peep through the deep-set casement windows, the air redolent with their scent. For all of us, the rose-covered cottage, nestled at the heart of the garden, is a place of contentment, snugness, and seclusion where happiness is forever and it is always time for tea.

HEAVENLY SCENTS

e have always needed the perfume of roses, not just to breathe in as we bend over a comely blossom, but to enrich and beautify our lives. For this reason, the rose's fragrance in all its variations has perfumed the pages of history. Books, letters, gloves, shoes, ribbons, and wigs, the ornaments of flirtation, vanity, and luxury, have carried the rose's perfume. The rose, above all other flowers associated with love and happiness, is the natural perfume for the home.

Rose water, civilization's first scent, made by steeping roses in liquid and oil, anointed the body and hair and cleansed the hands after feasting. At Persian banquets, it was drizzled over arriving guests. In the Emperor Nero's banqueting-hall, roses rained from the open ceiling and scented water was sprinkled from silver pipes over guests seated at the tables. Roses were used

This dainty pomander, easily created at home, is rich with the aroma of dewy roses and powdery vanilla. It is equally comfortable by the bed or as an informal centerpiece.

ROSEBUD & IVY POMANDER

Silvery-white lunaria pods
V-shaped florist's pins
Small yellow rosebuds
Hot glue
Pink rose petals
Tiny-leaved ivy sprays
Foam ball (3 or 4 inches)
4 drops rose oil
4 drops vanilla oil
2 drops rose geranium oil
1 drop jasmine

COVER THE the surface of a foam ball with lunaria pods. Then attach the rosebuds at 2-inch intervals by gluing the stems together and poking them through the foam. Intersperse with pink rose petals. Entwine the ball with ivy sprays, securing them at intervals with florist's pins. Mix half the essential oils to scent the pomander; save the rest for refreshing it later on.

ROSEMARY & ROSE SACHET

2 cups crushed dried
rose petals

2 cups crushed dried
rosemary leaves

1 tablespoon powdered orrisroot

1 tablespoon crushed cassia
buds or cloves

COMBINE THE petals, leaves, orrisroot (a fixative), and spices in a large bowl. Stir gently to blend, then set the bowl aside, tightly covered, for a month or so to allow the fragrance to develop. Uncover and toss or stir the mixture every few days to allow the the character of the sachet to intensify.

Fill small cotton bags or pieces of fabric with the mixture. Use a drawstring or colorful accent tie to secure the fabric. Tuck the sachets in closets and drawers.

Too beautiful to hide among the linens is this cushiony sachet. Concealed in a mist of gauze, tied with an organdy butterfly bow, is a gathering of rose petals ~ richly, and lastingly, perfumed damask or centifolia roses, with a sprinkling of lavender flowers. Plumped on top is a single, velvety fantasy rose

in medicines, salves, and potions in ancient Rome and during the Dark Ages. In Tudor times rose water was used to purify air and freshen clothing and other fabrics.

Today, many of these practices survive, though slightly altered in purpose. To transform a home into a bower of tranquility and repose, we burn perfumed candles for the soft light and fragrance they bring, we mist the air with room perfume when we are expecting guests or at night before we sleep. We hide sachets beneath our pillows; line desk drawers with fragrant papers so that our notes and letters wing their way with extra charm. With the perfume of roses around us, we ourselves bloom from within. Perhaps it is true that the scent of the rose is "the beauty of life itself."

SHADES OF HARMONY

To have a house whose rooms are the colors of roses is to live in a perfect day in June all year round; the colors of roses heighten our perceptions, lend us a buoyancy, a lightness of heart. Without a rose in sight, the sense of the flower will be there, soothing, caressing, affecting in tints of pale pink, peach, Tyrian rose, cream, lemon white, in undercurrents of wine, maroon, purple, silvered lavender. In colors that match the crumpled pink silk petals of "Felicité Parmentier"; the violets and mauves of "Honorine de Brabant"; the amber pink of "Perle d'Or"; the cream and peach of "Marchioness of Londonderry"; "Iceberg's" white blushed with pink; the sunshine yellow of "Lawrence Johnston";

Pastel shades of pink and cream are not the only rose colors to paint a room. This bedroom glows, very much as the rose itself does, with the vitality of a rich red wine. Overleaf: The generous bouquet of roses on the lace-draped refectory table is reflected in the color of the walls, painted a subtle, connoisseur's blend of white, cream, and the merest whisks of pink and yellow.

the pink touched with apricot of "New Dawn"; the pinks, lilacs, blue and deep magenta that give a smokiness to "Reine des Violettes"; even the pink, yellow, and cream combination of *chinensis mutabilis*.

To pick the colors that will give the deepest pleasure on the walls, the same method often suggested for choosing roses for the garden might be used: laying favorite roses together in groups to see how well they go together, then matching the colors with paint swatches. Even without fresh roses, colors might be picked from the pages of books of botanical drawings such as those of Redouté's *Les Roses*. Rose catalogues, too, might be read for the color descriptions alone, letting them fire the imagination for the house as well as the garden.

Whatever the choices, if they are from the same color family, the result will be a natural harmony, a flow from room to room that gives moving between them a joy akin to the joy we feel as we walk down the paths of a well-planned garden at dawn or in the early evening.

A Love Potion

A LOVE POTION, MADE

OF RED AND WHITE ROSE LEAVES

AND FORGET-ME-NOTS,

BOILED IN 385 DROPS OF WATER

FOR THE SIXTEENTH PART

OF AN HOUR, WILL, IF PROPERLY

MADE, INSURE THE LOVE

OF ONE OF THE OPPOSITE SEX,

IF THREE DROPS OF THE

MIXTURE ARE PUT INTO SOMETHING

THE PERSON IS TO DRINK.

A. STODDARD KULL

FLOWERS CAN SPEAK. This we have always known. Lilies, daisies, violets ~ each has its own vocabulary, accent, special turns of phrase. Of all them, however, roses are the most articulate. The petals hold everything that has ever been written about them, thought about them, every lament of a poet, every flutter of a lover's heart. A moment's listening and we hear the voice of the red rose calling "bravo!" or "courage!"; the almost inaudible white rose, vowing devotion. The rose is a peerless interpreter that, like a floral Cyrano, plays music with words, uttering impassioned phrases for the hesitant and shy.

It is the rose's power of speech that makes it a constant messenger. It is the reason that roses have through the ages mended quarrels, marked wedding anniversaries, celebrated births and birthdays, and enriched the funny, special-to-us moments in our lives that might otherwise have gone unnoticed as well as all-over-the-world holidays like Valentine's Day, Christmas with its rose of peace and joy, and New Year's with its rose of hope.

This ability to convey meaning is the reason the bride wears a rosy wreath or carries a gathering of roses as the ultimate symbol of love. In her hands, a rose bouquet is peerless. A bud taken from it and placed in the bridegroom's lapel has the most personal meaning of all.

The church, the tent, the house in which the wedding takes place, burgeoning with roses, reflects the wonder of the day. Perhaps miniature roses in pots or wooden tubs set off the entrance; clusters of roses among the ribbons cordon off the pews or mark the chairs reserved for the bridal family. On the poles that support a wedding canopy or hold the candles lining the aisle, roses become a bridal chorus twined in garlands of greenery or white satin ribbons. For a garden wedding in June, the month of roses, the poetry that is the rose perfumes the air. At the reception, the rose conveys the magic spell of fairy tales with standard roses placed on either side of the door. The wedding cake might be a spun sugar castle of roses. The wedding goblet, holding rose-colored champagne, may be tied with satin streamers studded with miniature roses or rosebuds. Great baskets can hold white roses in the midst of ebullient gatherings of other white flowers ~ peonies, lilacs, spires of foxglove, waxy anthurium.

A happy family celebration announces itself with a profusion of roses. On gold-rimmed turn-of-the-century Limoges dessert plates are hand-painted flowers so vivid and fresh-looking that they almost seem fragrant. The dining table itself is spectacularly sheltered in an antique tapestry rug.

Roses also speak for family love ~ the love of children for parents, expressed in the bouquet of roses or a rose-bearing tray for a special breakfast in bed on Mother's Day; a proud rose boutonniere on Father's Day; the exultant birthday bouquet. An array of roses is the bearer of good wishes and warmth presented to the new mother or brought to the new home. It is the perfect

thank-you after a dinner party. A rose speaks of youth in the single long-stemmed red rose carried by the graduate. It suggests the promise of the future in a chaplet that crowns the head of a young woman on her twenty-first birthday.

A small, quiet christening is all the more moving for the rose garlands, angelic as the baby's cheeks, tender as the mother's smile, that drape the chancel railing. At the gathering afterward, a rosy wreath on the door announces the event and welcomes visitors, as it did in ancient Greece. Inside, table or mantelpiece bears bouquets of baby pink and white roses. Tables in the garden are set with roses crowded in little baskets or glass bowls. This is truly a magical flower that echoes the words and wishes and unspoken blessings of all assembled. Life's most solemn moments, and its dearest, are deeper and sweeter for the words of roses. ❧

The Christmas rose glows amid the shining balls, green boughs, crystal goblets, and candlelight of this most festive of seasons. Fresh roses, fantasy roses of gold, roses on ribbon-trimmed hearts, together sing the age-old message of peace.

At a small, private reception at home, above and opposite, the

bride and groom's family and closest friends alone

share their precious moment. The bride's chair is ribboned in blue,

"like streamers in the painted sky," as was the custom in

Elizabethan England. Secured to the streamers are the white roses

that are the ultimate symbol of the bride.

Home is where roses rule. The formal luncheon table,

opposite, is crowned with blossoms in deep and pale shades of pink;

each place is marked by ribboned nosegays. A double

topiary picks up the centerpiece colors. In another setting, above,

tables drenched in heavy lace ~ a cutwork and a

needlepoint tablecloth ~ are caught up with nosegays of creamy

roses, cherries, rose hips, and variegated ivy.

A birthday breakfast is brought with smiles and a crystal

dish of roses on the tray, opposite, as a prelude to a day of cosseting.

Above, a rose lover's Mother's Day tea is set up by the window

overlooking her favorite view of the garden. The folding tray table is

decorated, appropriately, with decoupage botanical prints.

AT TABLE

The table can be a rose garden, a place where we can be certain of finding roses in beauty at any time of year. It is an unchanging climate, without frost, dampening rain, or drought. To cultivate such a garden, we may, first of all, bring in fresh flowers. On the formal table, a single long-stemmed red rose might be laid across the dinner plate or on the napkin. Small roses can be cinched together in a nosegay, a name card attached, to crown each place. Less formally, blossoms might be clustered in old-fashioned toothpick holders, cut-crystal salt shakers, small glass bottles, or jars of every description. Or a small assembly of miniature roses in their own pots might make its way down the length of the table. Perhaps at the

breakfast table, two or three small vases each hold a different flower ~ one white pansies, another forget-me-nots, a third pale apricot roses still dewy from the garden ~ or all three containers mingle the three kinds of flowers, no two bunches alike.

With dried roses, the flowers of summer can keep on blooming at the table, even when the last have retreated from the garden for their winter rest: encircling candle holders, clustered in tiny topiaries, standing in a bunch wrapped with wheat tassels or

A creamware box, like its eighteenth-century counterparts made by the renowned English potters, is topped with a molded rose, right. Opposite, a simple country cupboard shines with a garden's worth of floral motifs. Such is the power of the rose that though almost no two are alike, together they form a single bouquet of happy patterns.

leaves and tied with raffia or wired ribbon. They can be packed in small wooden crates or heart-shaped coeur à la crème molds. A single flower might come to rest on a napkin ring of entwined grapevine cuttings.

Roses also mesh with the fruits of the kitchen garden and the orchard, creating still lifes for our tables. However disparate the elements, the flower has a mysterious way of unifying them. English floral designer Constance Spry saw everything that grew in or out of the garden as a possibility. When preparing a mixed bouquet, she countered solid with slim flowers, heavy with light, adding branches of blossom, or, "better still," branches of fruit. A bouquet might include a trail of nasturtiums, a geranium, a branch of acorns or loganberry, a well-shaped thistle, a stem of red currants. In autumn, additions might include rose hips, seeds of sorrel, rhubarb, green artichokes or onion, ripe elderberries or blackberries, a few twigs of crab apple or small pears.

Still another way of enjoying the company of roses at the table is with rose-patterned linens: Imagine a white damask cloth woven with the image of the rose, or a lace edging frosting a linen tablecloth. Roses printed on cottons, embroidered on batistes, appliquéd on the gauziest organdy in shades of pink, violet, pure white, or pale yellow bring sunlight and spring to a luncheon on the grayest winter's day.

Roses often smile from glassware, flatware, and china as well. One of the earliest table porcelains was the eighteenth-century French Sèvres, the favorite of a king's favorite, Madame de Pompadour. Madame de Pompadour, who adored roses, not only pinned them on her brocades and in her fair hair, but as a patron of the Sèvres factories, she saw to it that her roses were made to last. The same meltingly soft blooms that French artist François Boucher painted with abandon in his portraits of Madame de Pompadour in the eighteenth century appeared in glory on many of the Sèvres pieces, surrounded by a bright pink since

come to be known as "rose Pompadour." Her successor in the king's affections, Madame du Barry, lent her name to another pink hue, "rose du Barry," which became a favorite color on nineteenth-century English pieces.

The rose also reigned on other European porcelains and chinas, such as those of

A napkin ring that is also a rosy wreath is more than prettily decorative; it becomes an important part of the joy of the table, opposite. Silverware, too, with handles gilded with ornate damask roses, above, needs no occasion to add a sense of celebration.

Meissen, Limoges, Strasbourg, and Mennecy. Molded roses formed the knobs and finials on the lids of teapots, tureens, and sugar bowls, and they festooned poetic figurines. By 1760, English potteries were supplying an avid public with rose-painted or rose-encrusted table services; among the great flower-laden chinas that emerged were Lowestoft, Plymouth, Bristol, Leeds, New Hall, Swansea, Derby, Coalport, Wedgwood, Coalbrookdale, and Spode. In the 1930s, English ladies who took tea found particular delight in Worcester's Blind Earl pattern with its raised rosebuds and rose leaves.

An array of contemporary cups is splendid with gilt and delicately painted roses, left. Below, the daintiest wisp of scalloped organdy becomes daintier still when embroidered with a rosy twig, so real-looking it might have been freshly plucked from the garden.

Today, whether in sets or as accents with other services, rose-decorated china brings a special flourish to the table. Even odd pieces garnered at sales or found in antique shops, with little in common except for their rosy theme, add a personalized touch, especially to the intimacy of breakfast or tea. In all its forms and interpretations, the rose lends its gift of grace to all who gather at table. 🌿

CHINTZWARE IN BLOOM

The rose is all smiles and hominess on the chintzware of the country table. There, it is at its most irrepressible, consorting with such innocents as bluebells and daisies and forget-me-nots, seeming perpetually ready for the joyful occasion ~ a picnic at the foot of the garden, a child's birthday party, a graceful afternoon tea, or a languid Sunday morning breakfast in bed.

Although the chintzware that is most sought after today dates from the 1930s to the 1960s, when its overall patterns became daintier and more dense, its origins go back some three centuries to the days when the ships of the East India Companies were returning to Europe with teas, spices, porcelains, silks, and a printed Indian cotton called

Fantastical birds perched among the roses, right, suggest this unmarked pitcher is a Victorian treasure. A chintzware must-have, opposite, is a Royal Winton stacking teapot in meadow-fair "Julia." The teapot, sugar bowl, cream pitcher, and lid all fit together in one easy-to-carry piece bound for the tea table.

chintz (probably, from the Sanskrit word *chint*, meaning "variegated") or calico. Its exotic patterns of fantastic birds, trees, and flowers, which were painted or printed on, and its inexpensiveness made it popular for both home and fashion. Leading English potteries such as Wedgwood, Derby, Chelsea, Worcester, and Bow began borrowing its motifs for their tableware. Soon birds flew, cornucopias poured, roses triumphed, lace

Like pocket-size gardens, three pitchers suggest cozy pleasures of the English cottage. From the left: "Royalty" by Royal Winton; a burst of spring flowers by the Myott Company; and blue and white roses with twining golden stems from Lord Nelson.

fluttered. At first, the cost of having every rose and leaf, every bird and butterfly painted by hand made the prices prohibitive for all but the finest manor houses. The development of transfer printing in the middle of the eighteenth century, however, made it possible for chintz-patterned china to become as much a part of the cottage as chintz itself. In this process, a kind of lithography, transfer sheets were pressed on engraved copper plates inked with ceramic color. The sheets were then hung like clothes on a laundry line to dry, then cut to fit the items they were intended to cover. Size ~ a mixture of glue and water ~ was brushed on the piece so that the pattern would stick when it was transferred. After the pattern dried, the paper was rubbed off with a damp sponge. The piece was glazed, then fired. If a lasting pattern was the primary object, it was transferred before the piece was glazed; if the brightness of the pattern was considered more important, the transfer was not done until the glazing process was completed.

The popularity of chintzware meant that virtually every country attempted its own version, but it was the English who met with the greatest success. Of all those who came to produce chintzware ~ James Kent, Shelley, Empire, Crown Ducal, Royal Albert, Lord Nelson, Keeling & Company, Crown Devon, and Midwinter, to name just some of the best known ~ none surpassed the output of Leonard Lumsden Grimwade. In 1855, he and his two eldest brothers began their business in a small shed in Stoke-on-Trent. By 1892, they were able to build a large factory, Winton Pottery, within minutes of the railway station to expedite their

A flower arranger in Royal Winton's "Cranstone" pattern is a study in roses echoing roses. This "ordinary, everyday" china became even more popular after the second World War because it was so bright and cheerful.

orders. More factories soon followed, among them the Rubian Art Pottery; Upper Hanley, or Brownfield's, Pottery; Atlas China; and Heron Cross Pottery. In 1928, the first Royal Winton pattern, "Marguerite," was produced; it was copied from a flowery cushion that Leonard Grimwade's wife embroidered.

Not only were these chintzware pieces, and those of other potteries, pleasingly patterned with a meadow's worth of gay flowers, they were made in an array of cunningly contrived shapes. Today's collectors eagerly look for demitasse coffee sets; stacking teapots; breakfast trays complete with teapots, creamers and sugars, cups, and toast racks. They search out small salad forks and spoons, lamp bases, biscuit barrels, baskets, bud vases, bonbon dishes, loving cups, sugar shakers, hot water bottles, and jardinieres; they fervently hope to discover a unique piece. Though some look far and wide for sets, many are happy to come home with odd pieces, putting together serendipitous combinations with plainer modern pieces or gilt-edged Victorian china. ❧

Musk Rose Water

Take two handfuls of your
Musk Rose leaves, put them into
about a quart of fair water
and a quarter of a pound
of sugar, let this stand and steep
about half an hour, then take
your water and flowers
and pour them out of one vessel
into another till such
time as the water hath taken the
scent and taste of the flowers,
then set it in a cool place
a-cooling and you will find it a
most excellent scent-water.

WILLIAM RABISHA
1675

THE CRAF

CRAFTSMEN'S FINGERS have always tried to capture the rose, to somehow possess its elusive essence. For as long as roses have been cultivated, they have been fashioned in paper, shaped in beaten gold and molded in porcelain, embroidered in vivid silks on tapestries, carved on wood, quilted on capacious coverlets, woven on luxurious carpets. The rose-obsessed Romans planted roses in fields that should have held grain and fruit trees, complained the poet Horace, and still they felt they hadn't enough; they went so far as to import fresh roses and paper roses from Egypt. The works of the Persian poets ~ often dedicated to the rose ~ were inscribed on a silky paper powdered with gold or silver, its margins decorated with the rose and the nightingale. The paper itself was tinted in shades of rose and sometimes scented with attar of roses. The Dutch flower painters of the late sixteenth, seventeenth, and early eighteenth centuries ~ perhaps

TED ROSE

the most famouse example is Jan Brueghel the Elder ~ made artisans conscious of the design potential of naturalistic roses. Cabinetmakers brought grace to drawing rooms by inlaying furniture with swags and bunches of roses in marquetry or on porcelain plaques. Potters brought grandeur to the table with roses on serving pieces from the factories of Strasbourg, Mennecy, and Limoges, each identifiable by its version of the rose. In the skilled hands of the potters of Meissen, figurines of loving shepherds and shepherdesses drowsed among roses. Porcelain roses held menu cards, and those who couldn't afford the real thing dipped roses in egg whites and sugar to make *roses en chemise* in imitation.

Over the centuries, ladies plied their needles ambitiously, embroidering roses on chair coverings, screen panels, bedcovers, even carpets, until in the eighteenth century they began more frivolously to compose roses out of beads, shells, and curled paper.

One of the most gifted artist-craftswomen was Mary Delany, who made what she called "paper mosaicks" by cutting flower petals and leaves from colored papers and pasting them on black cards. In the nineteenth century, weavers produced Berlin woolwork carpets, which were characterized by lush cabbage roses. The fabrics of English Arts and Crafts innovator William Morris and the wallpapers of illustrator Walter Crane repeatedly paid tribute to the humble five-petaled rose. In New England, women made rose blankets ~ white blankets that were woven on looms, then embroidered at the corners with rosette designs in colored yarns.

A modern variation on an old technique: glass-painting. The blown glass shade, shaped like an exploded flower bell, glows with luscious cabbage roses. The effect of the lamplight is to make this flower or that spring forward as the viewer moves around the table.

From these ideas of the past, we continue to take our decorative themes, adapting old methods to new uses. We translate a rosy detail from a piece of Stuart needlework to an embroidery canvas to make cushions or chair covers. For a stencil,

we trace a pattern such as those used by Scottish architect Charles Rennie Mackintosh to bring roses to a worn wooden table, a picture frame, a chair rail. We cut up old pictures of roses to cover a lampshade or screen in decoupage; frame rose prints to hang in an entry hall; use a rose-printed fabric to cover a diary or create a sachet pillow. We finish off gift packages with paper, fabric, or dried roses; tie them with rose-strewn French embroidered ribbon. We cover boxes in rosy paper, affix the image of a rose in sealing wax on letters. What was recognized by the craftsmen of the past we recognize still: The rose represents hundreds of beautiful associations we yearn to preserve and expand ~ the perfect days of June; a sweetheart's first bouquet; a walk in the garden after a rain. To keep the rose ever at hand, we make if we can, buy if we must, the flower that seems to speak to us alone. ❧

Moments when roses are not in bloom and the garden outside sleeps for the winter season can still be moments devoted to them by making them bloom forever in needlepoint. Then, too, as the needle pierces the canvas, the mind is free to roam among the flowers.

Furniture inlaid, painted,

or stenciled with roses has been an

important part of decoration

for centuries. The wardrobe, right,

and the transitional-

style commode, opposite, become

highly personal pieces

with their garnishes of blossoms

and sprays of roses.

The lucky browser in an antiques
shop may come upon a
beauty like the painted table, opposite,
its gentle roses speaking
of craftsmanship of times gone by.
Another link with the past
is porcelain-painting, left, once a
favorite pastime for
ladies who loved flowers and art.

The rose has been the subject of needlework since ladies

sat within castle walls stitching tapestries. Our roses today are more

likely to be set blooming on upholstery, above and opposite.

Overleaf: Life is truly a bed of roses on an accommodating chaise

longue in a rose print, made even more luxurious by

a needlepoint pillow and a ribbon-embroidered pink wool throw.

In a bedroom awash in light and roses, a Victorian counterpane,

opposite and above, hangs on the wall behind the bed like

a medieval tapestry. No attempt has been made to match the pillows

on the bed; instead, their common denominator is the rose

itself, embroidered in myriad ways. Even the candlestick on the

bedside table wears the flower on a tapestry bow.

IN SILK AND SATIN

The likeness of roses to the most luxurious fabrics we know is something few rose lovers fail to observe. "Silk," "satin," "velvet" ~ the words spring immediately to mind when gazing at the iridescent sheen and swirling petals of a rose. In *Mrs Dalloway*, Virginia Woolf wrote of the roses laid in wicker baskets at a florist's as looking fresh as "frilled linen clean from a laundry basket." And Vita Sackville-West said of old roses, "I think you should approach them as though they were textiles rather than flowers." To her, even the perfume of roses on the June air was velvet.

The resemblance between rose petals and gorgeous cloths has always motivated artisans and craftsmen to attempt to produce artificial roses whose beauty rivaled that of the living flower. Artificial roses were made by the Romans, Egyptians, and Chinese from various precious materials. Centuries later, the Italians introduced the art of flower-making into France, and from there it crossed the Channel to England. Rosettes and pompons, looped of ribbon, became the height of fashion everywhere, affected by both men and women. Shakespeare piled them on his hat and shoes, and assured his audiences that Hamlet wore them, too. The rage was such that in 1604, writer Francis Bacon said ruefully, "When roses in the garden grew / And not in ribbons on a shoe; / Now ribbon roses take such place / That garden roses want their grace."

The fashion had not subsided a century later. Gentlemen's court shoes, as well as the garters that were cinched below the knee (drawing the eye to a well-turned leg), were frivolously studded with rosettes. Gentlemen's toes twinkled with roses. An English visitor to the Swedish court of Gustavus III noted the women wore black dresses with puffed and slashed sleeves, their

Crimped and curled, a fantasy rose nestles in folds of silk next to a tool for flower-making. The tool, a nineteenth-century metal goffer, cups petals in imitation of the living rose. Little has changed in the artistry of crafting artificial flowers: The goffer is still used today.

red sashes centered with rosettes. The men, meanwhile, wore Spanish-style jackets and full breeches in black with red buttons and stripes, black cloaks edged in red satin, red satin waistcoats ~ and, fittingly, red satin roses on their shoes.

Even as paintings of roses grew more naturalistic ~ roving bees, dewdrops trembling on petals ~ so, too, did rose adornments. The rosettes of ribbon, more symbols than accurate depictions, faded in the presence of silk-petaled flowers so beautifully wrought they were almost indistinguishable from the real thing. Making these confections was the work of nuns in Italian convents, and of milliners and their young assistants.

Like other handwork, such as lacemaking and embroidery, flower-making at its best became an agreeable source of income for women. Some worked at home. Others sat together at tables in ateliers, laughing, talking, gossiping, while their deft fingers assembled the roses that would bedeck coquettish hats and be strewn on sweeping skirts of taffeta and satin. The fabric for the

These silk cabbage roses might have been washed with color by a master Impressionist. In flower-making, such petals, in tints a real rose might envy, are cut in graduated sizes and individually dyed to capture the ineffable subtlety of the flower itself.

roses was first brushed with starch, then cut into petals and individually dyed. Next they were laid between screens and left to dry for several days. It was at this point that they were passed along to the flower-makers. These women, holding the petals in the palms of their hands, applied a heated metal ball with a handle, which cupped, or "goffered," them. The petals were then crimped and curled with the fingers before being pasted to the center, the "pep," where the stem was attached. Once the petals and leaves were in position, the most skillful flower-makers arranged, or "branched," them to achieve the elegance that would make the flower irresistible.

What so beautifully adorned fashions eventually found its way into the home. For those without greenhouses, these fantasy flowers provided a note of unseasonal gaiety to their surroundings, a summery contrast

*R*ibbon roses, twined and stitched together
by gifted hands, may be attached to table and bed linens,
as well as used in a multitude of other personal
ways. The flowers above are formed of rolled French
wire ribbon. The snub-nosed bud ornamenting
a sachet pillow, opposite, is wrapped in lustrous satin.

perhaps to the falling snow outside. The Victorians nestled silk nosegays and bridal wreaths under bell jars for display on the parlor mantel. Today, silk roses might stand on a table in the foyer to welcome guests or on a pedestal in the living room; big, loose-petaled roses might bloom on tiebacks that draw aside the folds of a curtain, embellish a strip of tulle draped by a dressing-table mirror, or form a crown over a stream of netting falling behind a bed.

Anywhere a dried rose might charm, a fabric rose may do so as well. A small velvet rose attached to a ribbon becomes a book-mark. Gold, silver, or white roses turn a swag of greens or a Christmas wreath into magic. The bridesmaid's rose coronet becomes souvenir and decoration when hung on a bedroom wall after the wedding. Single silk roses rest, as if absently laid there, on a tabletop, or among cushions, or amid the books on a library shelf. The fantasy rose, like the rose in the garden it reflects, is a continuous reminder of living gracefully. ❧

HEARTS AND FLOWERS

On Valentine's Day, roses are essential. On that day, the rose reigns unchallenged, absolute monarch of the heart, the true queen of flowers, the symbol of passion, the promise of love. Whether a single, faultless flower or a nosegay with the dainty buds of the sweetheart rose; whether pink, white, or red roses pressed together in a heart-shaped basket; whether poised on a candy box or printed on a card, the rose is the lover's gift. With a rose extended in his hand, every man becomes a poet and the rose as sure a messenger to the heart as Cupid's arrow. Every love poem, in turn, becomes a valentine when roses are part of its theme, a paean to the beloved, her perfections compared (to her advantage) with the perfection of

For the sweetest missives, floral notepapers are a custom older than the rococo valentine card. The designs here are from a variety of antique sources, including etchings for a children's book and an old postcard. Overleaf: The cupid on an antique card carries his message of love anew, mounted on embossed paper.

the rose. "O My Luve is like a red, red rose / That's newly sprung in June," sang Robert Burns. Happily, there are as many different roses as there are kinds of love.

Even before the good Bishop Valentinus lent the day his saintly name, February 14 belonged to lovers. The ancient Romans, believing it to be the day that birds chose their mates, honored Lupercus, or Pan, the god of animal life, the guardian of Nature's secrets. Imitating the birds, a boy chose his mate by drawing lots for the name of the girl who would be his sweetheart for the year. The festival, bursting as it did from the darkness of winter, survived, though subdued, into the early Christian era, merging with the feast of St. Valentinus, martyred on February 14 in 270 A.D. By the fourteenth century, Valentine's Day had reemerged with all its original joyfulness. In France, lovers exchanged wreaths of roses, known as *chappelets verts à la Saint-Valentin*. By the seventeenth century, the day had become a part of English life and customs were carefully observed. Ordinary swains gave their

valentines treats and wore their love notes on their sleeves. The wealthier gave costly gifts. By the eighteenth century, an American suitor might slip a written valentine, sealed with a kiss and a dollop of red wax, under his lady's door. Loving fingers began creating more artful valentines using watercolors or pen and ink on letter sheets, shaping them with pinprick work or elaborate cutout patterns. Birds, hearts, angels, and twining roses carried the heartfelt, if sometimes clumsy, messages and often proposals of marriage.

Though the occasional hand-colored engraving or lithograph made its way from England, Americans for the most part continued creating their own. For an extra bit of polish, the sophisticated valentine maker used stationery with gilded edges or an appropriately embossed border and selected a verse from booklets published in England especially for the purpose.

At last, in the middle of the nineteenth century, the valentine came into full bloom. Outstanding among the artists who created them were Walter Crane and Kate Greenaway.

The Valentine's Day gift of chocolate, one of today's most favored tokens of affection, becomes a lasting treat in a china box swept round with a rosy wreath. To write as sweet a thank-you note, rose-strewn stationery awaits a loving hand.

Messages of the past paled before the new commercial valentines ~ sentimental, gilded, rose-embossed, encrusted with layers of perforated paper lace thick as icing, images of cupids, doves, dainty ladies, palazzos, swains with hats over heart, garlanded swans drawing loveboats, and roses, roses, roses. Valentines had stands, movable parts, foldouts of honeycombed red tissue paper, gauzy inserts that blurred everything in a romantic haze. The gorgeous cards might be cherished long after the sender had gone out of the valentine's life.

From bucolic revel and lottery for lovers, Valentine's Day has become one of our dearest holidays. Sweet, disarmingly simple, its demands are minimal, its requirements few. On Valentine's, we need do little more than smile or sigh, say three words, and offer the poet's tribute of a rose. ❧

Essence of Roses

Layer rose petals in a large stone
jar with sea salt and press
the layers well down. When the jar
is full, seal it and stand it in
a cool, shaded place for 40 days.

Turn the contents of the
jar into a cloth and strain off the
liquid, squeezing the cloth
gently to extract it all. Put the
essence into glass bottles
until they are two-thirds full.
Seal and leave to stand
in the sun for 25 to 30 days to
purify the essence.

THE BLOO

*T*HE ROSE HAS NO choice but to look noble, even sublime. For some 26 million years, it has inherited the earth. Millennia before man arrived, it was already scattered over the northern hemisphere in China, Japan, America, and Europe. In that same dark time, the rose began to hybridize, one species crossing with another, needing little more than a prehistoric bee dipping his feet in pollen or a breeze to produce some provocative new floral concoction. But the roses in Europe steadfastly refused to show themselves other than in reds, pinks, and white. Among these beautifully stubborn, early roses were the Damask rose; Rosa alba, a natural hybrid favored by the rose-besotted Romans; the hundred-leaved Provençal or cabbage rose; Rosa gallica; and the prickly moss rose. And more frustrating than this narrow range of colors, most of the beloved flowers bloomed only in spring, leaving the better part of ten months for its devotees to pine.

MING ROSE

Not until the early nineteenth century ~ influenced in part by the enthusiasm of Napoleon's Empress Josephine ~ did collecting and breeding begin to alter the course of the rose's history. The principal force behind the changes were the delicate roses of China. Their fragrances, unlike the heavier perfume of the roses in Europe, were light and ebullient. Since the scent of some resembled the odor of the boxes in which tea was imported from the Orient, they became known as tea roses. Far more important than their scent, however, the slender roses, with their loosely formed blossoms, had the gift of gifts: continual bloom.

This attribute, when the China rose crossed with other roses, tended to make their progeny bloom more frequently. The offspring of one such flower became the forerunner of the modern hybrid tea, as well as a popular beauty in its own right.

A second major change in the eighteenth century began

with the rediscovery of the five-petaled Austrian Yellow rose. Probably a native of Turkey and Persia brought to Europe by the Moslems in 1560, it produced, when bred with Scotch roses, double (having fifteen or more fully developed petals) yellow roses. Even better results followed a later cross between a Persian Yellow and a Hybrid Perpetual. Their seedling, the repeat-blooming Soleil d'Or, set the modern rose alight. From these and further crosses came most of the resplendent yellow, orange, and two-toned roses that grow in our gardens today.

The modern hybrid tea was the rose the world had been waiting for: a flower enriched in color and capable of keeping a garden in beauty virtually all year long. Rose gardens sprang up on a grand scale with row on formal row of bushes. At great houses, parterres were tricked out with elaborate geometric patterns; little rose trees, called standards,

The perfect complement to a gray-shingled Victorian house is an ethereal pink rose whose opulent clusters cast a gentle fragrance on the air. As is often the case, the buds are a deeper pink, the flower becoming paler as it opens. Even the bluish tint of the leaves intensifies their beauty.

guarded paths. Circular, square, and rectangular beds of roses were tidily enclosed in boxwood hedges. Soon after the first hybrid tea appeared in 1867, the old roses fell into neglect, their hardiness one of the few reasons they managed to survive at all.

By the 1880s, the great English gardener William Robinson began his campaign against the artifice of rose gardens designed to display the hybrid teas and nothing else. He argued that roses be returned to the garden itself, "not only in beds, but in the old ways ~ over bower and trellis and as bushes . . . so as to break up flat surfaces and give us light and shade where all is usually so level and hard. . . . As the bloom is beautiful in all stages and sizes, roses should be seen closely massed, feathering to the ground." Another English gardener, Gertrude Jekyll, also espoused the freer, more natural garden and the so-called old rose. As a way of learning what harmonies are best to plant in the

A time-honored method of caring for or reviving cut roses is to strip the lower leaves, then cut the stems again and submerge them in a pail filled with warmish water.

garden or to assemble in bowls, she suggested laying out cut roses in groups of two to four ~ "perhaps in some cool, shady place upon the grass" ~ and studying their effects in relation to each other. "Roses well assorted," she remarked, "are like a company of sympathetic friends ~ they better one another."

The work of the Dutch flower painters; Redouté; the Impressionists Manet and Fantin-Latour; and garden writers Robinson, Jekyll, and Sackville-West continue to inspire us to enjoy, on however much smaller a scale, the luscious beauty of the old rose, and of its elegant tea rose descendants. Choosing the resplendent offerings of rose growers, from the ancient five-petaled Eglantine to the sumptuous Victorian beauties and the peerless hybrid teas, we may conclude, with Miss Jekyll, on seeing her roses after the rain, "It is good to live, and all the more good to live in a garden."

An eighteenth-century-style French basket holds a covey of peach and apricot blooms garnered from the garden in the early morning. The same basket, lined and filled with moistened styrofoam and cut roses, will provide a glorious welcome near the front door.

A simple sign stenciled on
pine, right, indicates where the
gardener may be found
when friends come to call. The
luminous roses themselves
give precise directions. Opposite:
A vase brought into the
garden ensures that not a moment
is lost between cutting
and placing the flowers in water.

Even a humble container
shows off the glory of the rose,
opposite. An old green
Mason jar holds fresh gatherings
from the kitchen garden:
delicious roses and raspberries.
And no vase is so elegant
that it doesn't become
more so with the addition of two
or three white roses, left.

A FINE ARRANGEMENT

"n the history of flower arrangement . . . the name of Gertrude Jekyll . . . must always be outstanding," said garden writer Beverley Nichols. "Her classic *Colour Schemes for the Flower Garden* might have been written yesterday, for many of its lessons are still unlearned, but it was actually published in 1908, a year which marked the full tide of Edwardian vulgarity. . . . Onto this garish stage stepped Gertrude Jekyll, her arms laden with greys and whites and silvers, and many modest flowers that the Edwardians would not have deigned to notice in the country lanes where they bloomed so artlessly. . . . Most of [her bouquets], one suspects, were composed swiftly, from the first materials that came to hand."

The difference between Miss Jekyll and

Roses lend themselves to virtually any kind of arrangement. They may be put together with the careless nonchalance of a bouquet just gathered on a wander through a meadow, or become an element in a formal design such as this pavé heart.

others of her time becomes even clearer when we consider that those were the days when floral arrangements often rose to such heights and lavishness that guests at country house breakfasts had difficulty seeing each other for the columns of glass or silver, topped like exuberant wedding cakes with a floral outburst, while at dinner they might peer past fountains with pools of looking-glass, or carved blocks of ice.

Miss Jekyll's bouquets, by contrast, were overwhelming neither in size nor conception. To them, she brought an artist's eye and training, using the power of diagonals and the comfort of rounds, standing upright roses together with those that drooped, juxtaposing small single roses with big, blowsy ones, allowing flowers to sprawl, drift, follow their natural bent, and do in a bouquet many of the things they might do so triumphantly in the spacious reaches of a garden. She believed strongly in the "unintentional" arrangement of flowers. Her preferred style for a rose bouquet was to combine different varieties, ornamented

*O**f all the flowers, the rose seems the most adaptable;
not only does it look lovely in a wide variety of arrangements,
it can beautifully be combined with the unlikeliest
of flowers, buds, leaves, fruits, and vegetables. Here, a
freshly cut giant posy of roses is surrounded with coarse
green leaves and pointed with a few double narcissus.*

only by their leaves ~ springing branches of double Scotch briers with blossoms of single-petaled wild burnet, or long sprays of tight-petaled ramblers in the midst of fulsome Maiden's Blush. At times, however, she inserted sprigs of honeysuckle and small white pinks in lush bunches of Cabbage, Moss, and Damask roses; tucked sweet peas and fresh baby's breath, rosemary, or white pinks in among China roses; blended single and double roses with pansies; offered up white roses with delphinium and sea holly; branchy roses with clustering mountain laurel; tea roses with forget-me-nots. When the first bonfires crackled in the fields, she paired the rose's satin texture and voluptuous shapes with the reddish summer shoots of oak leaves, starry sprays of wild clematis, or dark ivy with its gray-green flower balls.

Before making an arrangement, Miss Jekyll advised keeping fresh-cut flowers in a galvanized pail of water for an hour or two. If they were to travel, she lined the bottom of a box with damp newspaper and packed the flowers tightly with fresh leaves ~ rhubarb, cabbage, lettuce, spinach, dock, or "any leaves that are large and cool and succulent." When the flowers arrived, the stems were to be cut again with a long slanting cut and quickly "plunged deep in warmish water right up to the flower and left all night."

Once the arranging began, containers as unpretentious as the arrangements were chosen: stout baskets, rough stoneware pottery, plain glass, Wedgwood creamware, pewter tankards, bronze pots, wine coolers, old glass finger bowls, silver cups and

In a plain glass vase, a cluster of roses with their own leaves has been given a delightfully diagonal lift. The shower of petals has not been tidied away, but left as a graceful reminder of the roses' ongoing life.

beakers, or the familiar blue and white Worcestershire or Rockingham china vases and bowls. "In many houses," remarked Miss Jekyll, "there are the remains of valuable old dinner services, reduced by breakage to a limited number of pieces that have found a home in glass cupboards, some of them so near the floor that they can scarcely be seen . . . Search should be made for these, for the salad-bowls, and especially the soup tureens, will be admirable for flowers, both cut and in pots."

To lend the flowers support, three flowerpots might be nested in a bowl, being sure to leave spaces for the stems. Wire netting or stiff greenery such as box or holly, pushed out of sight, also prevented heavy-headed roses from toppling over. The water was changed daily ~ fresh water being preferable, in Miss Jekyll's eyes, to the pinches of saltpeter, drops of ammonia and vinegar, or lumps of charcoal that others used. In putting the arrangements together, it was of utmost importance that the containers balance the flowers ~ the lift of the

flowers with the girth of the container ~ and that their colors complement the colors of the flowers and leaves. Even the color of the walls where the bouquet would be placed and the influence of artificial light on the flowers' tints were considered. Above all, the rose enthusiast was to learn to perceive the difference between harmonious and inharmonious effects.

The lessons Miss Jekyll and the old roses taught have, at last, been heeded. They have led to an escape from the rigidities that hybrid tea roses so long imposed, and they have made us willing occasionally to sacrifice those luxurious lengths of stem so we can focus on the intoxicating beauty of the blossoms alone. In a rose bowl, a glass globe designed to capture a dozen lanky hybrid teas, we now sometimes crowd at least as many roses, but roses cut short, in fullest bloom, in colors that pick up their hues from sunrise. Miss Jekyll has also made us willing to try exuberant bouquets that seem not to have been arranged at all but rather like those we might see in the chancel of an

Two of the most popular ways to present roses: The nineteenth-century silver nosegay holder, below, was once at home among the swirling crinolines of gala balls. One turn-of-the-century etched glass rose bowl, opposite, is always filled with the choicest blooms.

English country church: spilling over an almost invisible vase, carelessly mingling roses with Queen Anne's lace, peonies, trailing strands of ivy, hydrangeas, michaelmas daisies, whatever is growing in the garden. Miss Jekyll would be pleased. ❧

A POET'S LEGACY

ew people grow roses simply for their ornamental value; more do so out of helpless love. Even if first planted with cool calculation simply to "look pretty" or add a needed note of color to the garden scheme, roses have a way of moving into the gardener's heart and taking possession there. The first light of morning becomes a moment eagerly awaited, because it means being able to catch the rose when the dew still trembles on the leaves and the fragrance has only begun its sweet climb to full-day splendor. Darkness is the enemy that drives the gardener, unwillingly as a child led from the Christmas tree, indoors to rest.

These were the joys the American poet Anne Spencer knew. For her, writing and gardening merged until there was scarcely a

moment when one started and the other stopped. As she gardened, poetic phrases rang through her mind. As she wrote, often in the stillness of the night, the vision of her flowers kept her company.

The garden that Anne created at her home in Lynchburg, Virginia (the only place on earth to be, she believed: "Heaven's

The trellising of Anne Spencer's arbor, opposite, is wound with the deep red climber Crimson Glory, which makes its way across the archway. In the background are the pink-dipped blossoms of another climbing rose, Mme Grégoire Staechelin, a 1920s beauty (detail at right).

The popular climbing rose Blaze peeps over a wooden fence in the Spencer garden. It is one of thirty-five varieties that survived from the original garden, all dating from the Edwardian era to the Second World War.

Virginia when the year's at its Spring, " she wrote) was a constant reference point and solace ~ "half my world." Having been discovered by the literary world in the 1920s, her home became the meeting place of such leading American artists as Langston Hughes and Marian Anderson. Anne clung to the reality of her green sanctuary while feeling she was sometimes drowning in the constant conversation that surrounded her and her guests. The passion she felt for her garden, which surrounded the little cottage where she wrote, surely informed the lines in "Before the Feast of Shushan": "Garden of Shushan! / After Eden, all terrace, pool and flower recollect thee: / Ye weavers in saffron and haze and Tyrian purple, / Tell yet what range in color wakes the eye . . ."

In the long, narrow garden, planned along the classic English pattern, were poppies, nasturtiums, tangles of wisteria "dripping with the heavy honey of spring," and especially roses. On the desk where Anne wrote most of her poetry, with its handy scraps of paper, pen stand, family photographs, well-thumbed books of poetry, flower catalogues, packets of seeds waiting to be planted, and an old lamp with a capacious wicker shade for midnight writing, were sure to be, in season, trusses of roses casting their fragrance before her.

Anne Spencer's beloved garden is alive and flourishing again today. The dogwood, English boxwood, iris, and peonies have been brought back to strength by a local garden club. The pendulous wisteria, humming with bees, hangs over the cottage door, as it did when Anne came down the path. Old favorites such as American Beauty, Blaze, Mme Grégoire Staechelin, and Aloha reach high over an arbor, fall in tumultuous profusion over the fence. The scene is an exuberance much like Anne's poetry itself, flowers lifting to the sun she adored, making a poem for the eyes. ❧

ENDURING BEAUTY

ried roses are one of the most delicious ways to surround ourselves with roses. For centuries, they have succored the winter-weary and scented the home. A lingering breath of the rose's perfume, the tint of a dried petal bring with them a warming recollection of the sun's effulgence.

Whether we preserve the whole flower or just the petals, dried roses are a treasury to draw from and to share. There will be rosebuds to press into a tiny terra-cotta pot as a gift for a newborn baby, rosebuds to encircle a candlestick or to pin to a gauzy curtain. There will be roses to loop in garlands on the Christmas tree; roses for the tea table; a single rose for the breakfast tray.

With dried roses in sachets, linens become a delight to lift from cupboard

One of the rose's most natural floral complements in color, shape, and scent is lavender. Here, a shock of dried lavender flowers, bowed with French wire ribbon in a champagne shade, springs from among pink roses in a brass container.

shelves; scented sheets almost ensure sweet dreams. A porcelain bowl of potpourri, set on a polished wood table or windowsill, is an invitation to the fingers to riffle through, releasing the petals' fragrance once more.

Dried roses have long played a vital part in housekeeping. In the Middle Ages, sweet bags, or sachets, combated impure air, helped prevent moths, and even, it was believed, fought illness. Embroidered, beaded, and beribboned, they hung on bedposts and chairs or were worn inside the corsage of a gown. To make sweet bags, as well as pot-pourris, rose water, and other cosmetics, ladies and their maids gathered in the still room, a special room in great houses that was set aside for the purpose. The humblest cottage had its muslin bags or open boxes where herbs and flowers from meadow and garden exuded fragrance as they warmed near the fireplace.

By the eighteenth century, increasing trade with the East encouraged a more lavish hand with a variety of spices. A pot-pourri of Damask roses, white jasmine, deep

Ever-blooming rose blossoms have been freeze-dried, interspersed with eucalyptus buds, and piled into mossy terra-cotta flowerpots for year-round delectation, below. More classic approaches to dried flowers, opposite, are roses pressed close together into topiary trees and mounded high in flowerpots.

blue lavender, and silvery wisps of oakmoss, for instance, was made more lasting with powdered cloves, allspice, and orrisroot. Potpourris became so popular that porcelain bowls with pierced and ornamented lids were designed specially to hold them.

Though flowers and herbs gradually lost some of their medicinal uses, the tradition of drying roses has endured. If the

blossoms are intended for decoration, the roses (preferably red, yellow, or orange) are picked in midmorning, after the dew has evaporated and before the sun starts to drain

Garden Rose & Lavender Potpourri

1 cup pink rose petals
¼ cup pink rose buds
½ cup lavender flowers
1 cup blue delphinium blossoms
1 cup rose geranium leaves
4 tablespoons orrisroot powder
5 drops rose oil
2 drops lavender oil

I N   A   L A R G E   B O W L, mix together all the ingredients, stirring gently until they are blended. Cover the bowl tightly and set it aside for at least one month. Uncover and gently toss the mixture every few days to ensure that the aroma develops.

Words invent themselves and communication flows when thank-you notes, invitations, and letters are written on a delicate leaf of stationery and the air is filled with the light scent of fresh roses. A bowl of potpourri, blossoms resting on top, deepens the fragrance.

their colors. Then they are tied in small, loose bunches and hung upside down in an airy place away from the light, or laid side by side in a tray and covered with silica gel.

If the petals alone are to be preserved, they can be spread on a sieve, on muslin, or on thin paper, then placed in a warm spot (even a cool/warm oven), so that they dry quickly and retain as much fragrance and color as possible.

Most potpourri recipes call for a combination of the vigorously scented Damask rose and whatever herbs and spices are most pleasing. A good basic mixture can be made in the following proportions, according to England's Herb Society: To every 2 quarts of dried petals and herbs, add ½ ounce each of salt, orrisroot powder, cinnamon, nutmeg, cloves and mace, and ¼ ounce each of benzoin and olibanum. A few drops of oil of roses, oil of geranium or some other essential oil such as jasmine, musk, coriander, rosemary, or eucalyptus, can be added. When the fragrance begins to fade, a potpourri reviver or more drops of essential oil can be put in.

PHOTOGRAPHY CREDITS

1	Pierre Chanteau	49	Toshi Otsuki	96	Toshi Otsuki
2	Steve Cohen	50-51	Kari Haavisto	97	Toshi Otsuki
4-5	Zeva Oelbaum	52-53	Toshi Otsuki	99	Luciana Pampalone
6-7	Toshi Otsuki	57	Toshi Otsuki	100	Wendi Schneider
9	Tina Mucci	58	Toshi Otsuki	102	Wendi Schneider
11	William P. Steele	60	Toshi Otsuki	103	Pierre Chanteau
12-13	Toshi Otsuki	61	Toshi Otsuki	105	Toshi Otsuki
16	William P. Steele	62	Toshi Otsuki	106-107	Steve Cohen
19	Pierre Chanteau	63	William P. Steele	108	Pierre Chanteau
20	Toshi Otsuki	64	Pierre Chanteau	110-111	Michael Skott
22-23	Toshi Otsuki	65	Toshi Otsuki	114	William P. Steele
24	William P. Steele	66	Tina Mucci	117	Doug Foulke
25	Pierre Chanteau	67	Toshi Otsuki	118	Toshi Otsuki
26	William P. Steele *(left)*	68	Steve Randazzo	120	William P. Steele
26	Toshi Otsuki *(right)*	70	Toshi Otsuki	121	Toshi Otsuki
27	Toshi Otsuki	71	Toshi Otsuki	122	William P. Steele
28	William P. Steele	72-73	Steve Cohen	123	Nicolas Millet
29	Pierre Chanteau	73	Hedrich Blessing	125	Carlos Spaventa
30-31	Jeff McNamara	74	Starr Ockenga	126-127	Carlos Spaventa
32	Toshi Otsuki	75	Starr Ockenga	129	Carlos Spaventa
33	Pierre Chanteau	76-77	Starr Ockenga	130	Katrina De Leon
34	Gross and Daley	79	Starr Ockenga	131	Hedrich Blessing
35	William P. Steele *(top)*	80-81	Toshi Otsuki	132	Toshi Otsuki
35	Pierre Chanteau *(bottom)*	85	Toshi Otsuki	133	Toshi Otsuki
36	William P. Steele	86	William P. Steele	134	Toshi Otsuki
37	Pierre Chanteau	88	William P. Steele	137	Toshi Otsuki
39	Tina Mucci	89	Steve Cohen	138	Scott Morton
40-41	William P. Steele	90	Pierre Chanteau	139	William P. Steele
42	William P. Steele	91	Toshi Otsuki	141	Pierre Chanteau
45	Luciana Pampalone	92	Gross and Daley	143	William P. Steele
46	Pierre Chanteau	93	Steve Cohen	144	Toshi Otsuki
		94-95	Pierre Chanteau		

Front and back endpapers William P. Steele